THE GOLDEN RULES OF INVESTING

Start Young, Get Rich

Mark K. Bonhard

Kara Wilson, Editor
www.emergingink.com

To Pat, who has shared life's moments and supported
my journey for 55 years.

FOREWORD

If you are in high school or beginning your journey as a young adult, *read this book*.

Mark has bought his extensive business and financial experience and expertise to the complex topic of personal finance. *The Golden Rules of Investing* delivers an easy-to-read and understandable approach to creating a financial road map for your life.

So much has been written on these topics but so little on how to get started. By following Mark's advice, creating a plan, and sticking to it, you will be the master of your financial life. I recommend this book to everyone—teenagers, young adults, parents, and anyone looking to grasp the big picture of personal finance and investing.

As he clearly articulates, the earlier you get started, the better.

Good luck on your journey to financial independence!

Joseph P. Heider
President of Cirrus Wealth Management

Introduction

When most of us think of becoming rich or wealthy, we think of people like Elon Musk, Jeff Bezos, or Bill Gates. Or perhaps we dream of winning the lottery. But in this book, I want to define rich as "having enough in investments that work becomes optional."

You do not become "rich" when you've accumulated a certain amount of money. It is different for every person and varies based on an individual's lifestyle and cost of living.

Although this book is for teens, the advice presented applies to any investor with long-term financial goals.

Albert Einstein became famous for his Theory of Relativity as well as his many other contributions to modern science. While the genius of his ideas may not seem to have much practical application to our modern lives, the following quote assures otherwise:

Compound interest is the eighth wonder of the world. He who understands it earns it; he who doesn't pays it.

As I look back at my 30-plus years in financial services and my own life, I think about how helpful it would have been to have learned at an early age what follows here.

All aspects of money—investing, financial planning, saving, budgeting, taxes, etc.—are complex. For that reason, I have included ideas that apply to all ages and attempted to keep everything simple.

Financial literacy is crucial to your financial health and future. Without a solid understanding of the fundamentals of finance, such as compound interest, you will not only struggle to build wealth but quite possibly be taken advantage of by corporations and financial companies touting cheap ploys to earn your business.

Building wealth is a long-haul game. It's not something that happens overnight or even in a year. It is a skill and an innate comprehension of wise saving and spending practices.

This book details the steps needed to begin accumulating wealth and to set up your future self for success.

Retirement and old age are often referred to as the "Golden Years." In theory, at that time in an individual's life, a person has accumulated sufficient money, is collecting Social Security, has fewer responsibilities, and can lead a life of leisure and travel. I will make the case that the Golden Years of Investing are the earliest possible years. Money put away in your teens has a greater impact on creating wealth than money put away in later years.

1

FINANCIAL LITERACY

As a father—and now a grandfather—I have enjoyed telling bedtime stories to the children in my family. It has become habit that my nighttime tales feature a young boy and a girl. Some of the stories detail funny happenstances; others contain life lessons. Here is one for you!

In a little house by the edge of the woods lived a family with two children named Willie and Suzie. Willie was the older of the two. He was a happy, carefree lad who instigated most of the trouble that occurred in their formative years. Although more reserved and serious than her older brother, Suzie was also a content child.

Willie loved playing sports and video games and spent time hanging out with friends. Suzie did some of that as well but mostly enjoyed reading books. At 13, Suzie started babysitting to earn money. The only money Willie had was from the allowance he earned by doing chores around the house. Their parents encouraged them to save portions of their money. Suzie paid attention, but Willie blew through his allowance every week.

For the first two years, Suzie earned $500 each year from babysitting and saved half of it ($250). When she was 15 and 16, she doubled her income to $1,000 a year, again saving half of it ($500). At the age of 17, Suzie moved from babysitting to working at a clothing store which allowed her to save $1,000 each year. She continued this job through high school and college. After graduating college, she started her first full-time job.

Suzie put away $2,000 per year for the rest of her working career which she ended at age 67. At the suggestion of her father, the savings were put into an investment account and invested in equities (a.k.a. stocks).

To celebrate her 67th birthday, Willie invited Suzie to lunch. During lunch, Willie asked Suzie, "What are your plans now that you are not working?"

She smiled. "I plan to buy a second home in a warmer climate near a beach and to take at least three long vacations each year in different parts of the world."

Willie's expression went blank. He was silent for a long time. Finally, he meekly asked, "How can you possibly afford to do that? You have never had a high-paying job in your life. How can you possibly afford to do all that?"

Suzie explained, "I have been investing since I was 13."

As she outlined what she had done over the years, Willie—who was pretty good at math—grabbed a paper napkin and added up the amounts.

"Hah!" he laughed. "You must have won the lottery and not told me!"

Suzie gave a little shrug. "Nope."

"Come on. I crunched the numbers. Look, you've only saved a total of $95,500. That is not enough money to do what you are planning."

Once again, Suzie just smiled. "Well, you have the amount I put away figured correctly, but I now have about $2,000,000 in my investment account."[1]

Willie's jaw dropped.

---

[1] Suzie's hypothetical results are based on the historic returns in the equity markets of about 10% annually. Historic rates are just that—historic. They should not be taken as what future results may be.

Financial Independence

We support ourselves and our family by working, thus earning money. My aim in this book is to guide you to accumulate enough money so that work becomes *optional*. That is, you have enough money in your investments that you can support your desired lifestyle just from what your investments provide. This is **financial independence**!

This does not, however, mean that you retire or stop working. It means you can stop if you want to stop. Bill Gates and Warren Buffett still work. Do they *have* to work? No! They work because they want to.

One of the most important concepts in financial literacy is what Albert Einstein referred to as the "eighth wonder of the world." **Compound interest** is the interest that is earned on interest in a given period, usually measured in years.

Let's pretend that, at 13 years old, Suzie invests $250 which, in the first year, earns her 10% interest.

Ten percent of her total equaled $25. As a result, she had the original $250 plus $25 for a total of $275. In the next year, she receives another 10%, which brings her earned interest to $27.50. Again, the $25 is interest on her original investment. The extra $2.50 is interest *on the interest* she received in the first year, otherwise known as compound interest.

For the rest of her life, she *doesn't* invest another cent into her Roth IRA, a type of investment account. She only lets that $250 accumulate interest.

Here's a table to help you keep track of her progress, assuming a 10% interest compounded annually:

Age	Investment	New Total	10% Interest	End-of-Year Balance
13	+$250	$250	$25	$275
14	-	$275	$27.50	$302.50
15	-	$302.50	$30.25	$332.75
16	-	$332.75	$33.28	$366.03
17	-	$366.03	$36.60	$402.63
18	-	$402.63	$40.26	$442.89
19	-	$442.89	$44.29	$487.18
20	-	$487.18	$48.72	$535.90
66		$39,061.81	$3,906.18	**$42,967.99**

Lump Sum Future Value Calculator

Calculated future value is $42,967.99

The future value was calculated lump sum deposit of $250.00. Interest was calculated using a 10% rate of return for 54 years, compounded annually.

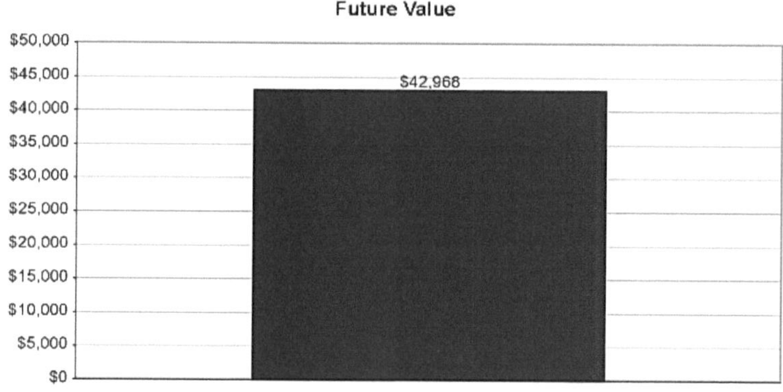

Results Summary	
Initial deposit amount	$250.00
Start date	6/16/2023
End date	6/15/2077
Dates span a period of	54 years
Rate of return	10% compounded annually
Future value	$42,967.99

Figure 1 With the Permission from KJE Computer Solutions, Inc. "Lump Sum Future Value Calculator," Dinkytown.net, June 16, 2023, https://www.dinkytown.net/java/lump-sum-future-value-calculator.html.

This repeats indefinitely—or until she stops investing or starts withdrawing. This investment alone, growing at an average annual rate of 10% for 54 years, would amount to **$42,967.99**.

Bank Accounts & Bonds

You may be asking, "What is investing and how does this work?" Simply put, investing is giving your money to someone or an entity for a given period with the expectation that it will be returned plus some as compensation for the use of your funds. You can loan money to banks, government agencies, or companies.

When you put money in a savings account at a bank, the bank pays you interest for the use of your money. The bank makes its money by loaning your money out at a higher interest rate than they are paying you on your savings account.

When you invest in **bonds**, "you are lending to the issuer, which may be a government, municipality, or corporation."[2] During that time, you receive interest; upon its conclusion, your principal (your original amount) is returned.

Below are a couple of examples regarding bonds.

Lake Erie to Canada

The state of Ohio decides that it needs to build a bridge across Lake Erie to Canada. It wants to improve trade with Canada and will collect tolls for use of the bridge. Because the state has no money in its budget to finance the project, it issues bonds to generate the funds to build the bridge. The state believes it can collect enough in tolls to pay off the bridge in 20 years. Ohio will then attempt to sell 20-year bonds to

---

[2] Investor.gov, "Bonds," U.S. Securities and Exchange Commission, Accessed June 1, 2023, https://www.investor.gov/introduction-investing/investing-basics/investment-products/bonds-or-fixed-income-products/bonds.

investors. The interest rate it will pay will be determined by the market at the time.

Distribution Center Purchase

Hit 'Em Straight, a large distributor of all things golf, needs to buy two more distribution centers for their growing company. The cost of the centers will be $5,000,000 each. The company's number crunchers tell them that having these centers will add enough additional sales and cost savings to generate an extra $1,200,000 in profit.

Hit 'Em Straight does not have enough cash to fund this but thinks that it can sell bonds to finance the new buildings. The bonds, given the current market, would pay 7%. Seven percent of $10,000,000 is $700,000. The company decides to move forward with the centers.

Loaning money to the U.S. government is the safest loan of all. If the 10-year treasury note is paying 4% interest, this affects what you, an investor, can expect to receive in interest from all other loans. This is why Hit 'Em Straight must pay 7%.

Loaning money to Hit 'M Straight is riskier than loaning money to the U.S. government. If Hit 'Em Straight tried to sell their bonds at 4%, no one would buy them since they would be compensated for the extra risk.

Stocks

Another form of investing is buying a piece of ownership of a company. You do not receive interest. In this case, you are expecting the company to pay you a share of their profits, which are referred to as dividends. In addition, you expect the company to grow thus increasing the value of your ownership. Ownership of companies comes in the form of shares of stock. We will focus on stock ownership as the main investment for young people. Historically, stocks have performed at a much higher return level than other types of investments.

Willie's Wonders

Willie's two favorite foods are doughnuts and bacon. Willie decides he is going to start a business making bacon-flavored doughnuts. He sets up shop in his family's kitchen and gets a website for Willie's Wonders (the name of his new company). Orders start rolling in. In the first year, the new company earns $20,000 after all expenses. Willie knows he has a hit on his hands, but there's a dilemma. He needs more appliances than a home kitchen can provide. In addition, it appears that he will need to hire staff.

He goes to several banks for a loan but gets turned down. They tell him that he is too small and that he does not have a long enough track record. Willie decides to get investors. He thinks he needs $100,000 to cover buying baking equipment and supplies, rent, and hiring staff.

He issues 1,000 shares of Willie's Wonders, keeping 200 for himself and selling the other 800 shares at $1,000 each. Willie will use the $20,000 he earned to sell ownership shares to generate the balance.

You buy one share. Willie's Wonders goes viral. The world cannot get enough bacon-flavored doughnuts. After all expenses, the company earns $100,000. Willie decides to keep $50,000 to help hire additional staff and pays out the rest in dividends. Because you bought a share, you receive $50 for your 0.1% ownership of the company. Also, the value of the company has increased. If you were to sell your share, it should sell for more than the $1,000 you invested. The value of the company, thus its shares of stocks, has increased by the amount of profit it made minus the dividends it paid.

In a simple world, your share would be worth $1,050. Stock prices reflect the expected future dividends and growth of a company. Given Willie's Wonders' 500% growth in earnings from the prior year and the potential for this trend to continue, stock buyers might be willing to pay more than $1,050.

If, on the other hand, Dunkin Donuts and Krispy Kreme announce that they are adding bacon-flavored doughnuts to their product lineups, you might not be able to sell your share at all. In essence, this is why stocks have a higher return than bonds.

What I described in the above scenario is a *privately*-traded company and a *private* transaction. The stock market is made up of much larger companies than Willie's Wonders and the shares of these companies are publicly traded. If Willie's Wonders continues to grow exponentially and needs even more funds, it could go "public" and attempt to sell its shares in the public market.

United States Treasury bonds and debt instruments of the Treasury, referred to as notes and bills, are considered by some as risk-free investments or as the least risky of all possible investments. The 10-year Treasury note is a debt obligation issued by the United States government with a maturity of 10 years upon issuance. A 10-year Treasury note pays interest at a fixed rate once every six months and pays the face value to the holder at maturity. It is backed by the United States government.

Currently, 10-year treasury notes pay 3.64% interest. But it carries two risks—inflation and liquidity risk. If inflation is running at 5% annually and you receive 3.74% in interest, you are losing 1.26% in buying power per year.

If you must sell the note before it matures in 10 years, you might not receive all your principal. Despite this, the obligations of our government remain the standard for safe investments.

When you purchase stock and ownership in a company, you take on more risks, like business risk. The company might have ineffective management, causing you to lose all that you invested. Or the economy could go into a recession which might also produce the same results even if the management is top-notch.

Another threat to your stock purchase is competition. Like Willie's Wonders, other companies will see one entity's success and try to copy it.

Investing in stocks is inherently riskier than investing in bonds. The prudent investor will only take on additional risk if they can expect higher returns.

2
THE GOLDEN RULES OF INVESTING

Rule 1: Pay Yourself First

Pay yourself first, then tailor your spending to what is left. If you are unwilling to do that, the rest of what follows will not matter. You have my permission to stop reading.

The best way to make sure you pay yourself first is to create and adhere to a budget. This means listing all your anticipated expenses first. The nice part of living at home is that, in most cases, you will have very few or no expenses. You can learn about paying for food, clothing, and insurance later. Your expenses will just be the things that you buy for yourself.

Let's bring Suzie back into the mix. Remember, Suzie began babysitting once a week for $25 at 13 years old. Ever the pragmatist, Suzie realizes that she might miss a week or two throughout the year due to holidays or illness, so, she figures two weeks' deduction in her math.

If she works the remaining 50 weeks, she will earn $1,200 during the year. Her parents pretty much pay for everything. Still, when she goes to the mall with friends, she would like to be able to buy something on her own. She makes a simple budget—spend $600 and invest $600.

This represents what you earn monthly or annually.

This depicts the way most people try to save—spend first and save what's left. The problem with this system, however, is that often little or nothing is left for savings.

The successful method of saving is to pay yourself first and then spend what is left.

Rule 2: Have an Emergency Fund

Although you might not need an emergency fund at this point in your life, unexpected expenditures can arise. You want to splurge on a prom dress; you end up eating out with your baseball team upon winning an underdog game; your parents didn't give you enough money to pay for additional meals on an out-of-state band trip. Things happen.

Suzie rented an apartment after graduating college. The family always had a dog, and she decided she would like one of her own. Off to the local rescue village she went. That afternoon, she returned with a mutt that she named Winston. About a year later, Winston developed a health issue that required surgery. The vet bill was $5,000. Suzie was upset but not devastated. In addition to regular investments into her Roth IRA, she had set aside additional money in a savings account.

Without this emergency fund, Suzie might have had to stop her investments. There went a big chunk of her $2,000,000. Assuming that she is 23 and she skipped two or three months of investing, her result at 67 would be about $300,000 less. Remember Einstein's eighth wonder of the world—compound interest.

Rule 3: Understand and Accept Risk

We live with risk every day of our lives. We drive a car knowing we could get into an accident. We exercise or play sports knowing we could be injured. What are the risks involved in investing? Are there ways to lessen the risk?

When you invest, you have the option to explore different asset classes. An **asset class** is a category for investments with the same characteristics. Examples of asset classes include:

- ☞ U.S. Stocks
- ☞ International Stocks (from developed nations such as the European Union, Japan, and S. Korea)
- ☞ Emerging Markets (like China, India, and Brazil)
- ☞ Commodities (gold, silver, oil, etc.)
- ☞ Fixed Income (bonds, savings accounts)

The Willie and Suzie tale uses one asset class portfolio (U.S. stocks) and the historic return for stocks. Historic returns are the returns a particular asset class has had over a long time. In given years, an asset class may perform differently than its average, or the asset class will revert to that average. The historic return for U.S. stocks has been about 10% as tracked by the S&P 500 with dividends being reinvested.[3] The historic return for U.S. bonds over the same period has fluctuated between 4% and 6%.[4]

---

[3] James Royal, "What Is the Average Stock Market Return?" NerdWallet, May 30, 2023,
https://www.nerdwallet.com/article/investing/average-stock-market-return#:~:text=stock%20market%20return%3F-
,The%20average%20stock%20market%20return%20is%20about%2010%25%20per%20year,other%20years%2C%20it%20returns%20less.
[4] Portfolio Management, "Why Diversification Matters: Markets Rarely Deliver 'Average' Returns," Charles Schwab, July 22, 2019,
https://intelligent.schwab.com/article/markets-rarely-deliver-average-returns#:~:text=When%20people%20think%20about%20investing,return%20for%20bonds%20was%206.1%25.

Yearly & Annualized Returns for Different Asset Classes

	LARGE CAP	SMALL CAP	BONDS	REAL ESTATE	INT'L
1977	7.16	25.38 ◄	3.04	22.42	18.06
1978	6.57	21.42	1.39	10.34	32.62 ◄
1979	22.33	43.07 ◄	1.93	35.86	4.75
1980	31.87	38.60 ◄	2.71	24.37	22.58
1981	5.10	2.03	6.25 ◄	6.00	-2.28
1982	20.31	24.95	32.62 ◄	21.60	-1.86
1983	22.13	29.13	8.36	30.64 ◄	23.69
1984	4.75	7.30	15.15	20.93 ◄	7.38
1985	32.26	31.05	22.10	19.10	56.16 ◄
1986	17.87	5.68	15.26	19.16	69.44 ◄
1987	2.93	-8.80	2.76	3.64	24.63 ◄
1988	17.26	25.02	7.89	13.49	28.27 ◄
1989	30.43 ◄	16.26	14.53	8.84	10.54
1990	-4.21	-19.48	8.96 ◄	-15.35	-23.45
1991	33.04	46.04 ◄	16.00	35.70	12.13
1992	8.93	18.41 ◄	7.40	14.59	-12.17
1993	10.18	18.88	9.75	19.65	32.56 ◄
1994	0.39	-1.82	-2.92	3.17	7.78 ◄
1995	37.77 ◄	28.45	18.47	15.27	11.21
1996	22.45	16.49	3.63	35.27 ◄	6.05
1997	32.85 ◄	22.36	9.65	20.26	1.78
1998	27.02 ◄	-2.55	8.69	-17.50	20.00
1999	20.91	21.26	-0.82	-4.62	26.96 ◄
2000	-7.79	-3.02	11.63	26.37 ◄	-14.17
2001	-12.45	2.49	8.44	13.93 ◄	-21.44
2002	-21.65	20.48	10.26 ◄	3.82	-15.94
2003	29.89	47.25 ◄	4.10	37.13	39.59
2004	11.40	18.33	4.34	31.58 ◄	20.25
2005	6.27	4.55	2.43	11.80	13.54 ◄
2006	15.46	18.37	4.33	41.81 ◄	26.34
2007	5.77	-1.57	6.97	7.39	11.17 ◄
2008	-37.60	-33.79	5.24 ◄	-48.16	-43.38
2009	28.43	27.17	5.93	37.13 ◄	31.78
2010	16.10	26.85 ◄	6.54	19.63	7.75
2011	1.50	-4.18	7.84 ◄	8.46	-12.14
2012	16.42	16.35	4.21	27.73 ◄	17.32
2013	33.11	38.82 ◄	-2.02	5.67	22.78
2014	13.24	4.89	5.97	15.02 ◄	-4.90
2015	0.92 ◄	-4.41	0.55	-0.79	-0.81
2016	12.05	21.31 ◄	2.65	4.06	1.00
2017	21.69	14.65	3.54	10.36	25.03 ◄
2018	-4.78	-11.01	0.01 ◄	-5.63	-13.79
2019	31.43 ◄	25.52	8.72	21.91	22.01
2020	20.96 ◄	19.96	7.51	9.04	7.82
2021	26.45 ◄	14.82	-1.54	26.09	11.26
2022	-19.13	-20.44	-13.01 ◄	25.09	-14.45
Annualized Return 1977-2022	11.36	12.18	6.64	11.25	8.57
Annualized Standard Deviation 1977-2022	15.35	20.32	5.34	15.83	16.60

Figure 2 Russell Investments. 2023. "Comparing Single-Asset to Multi-Asset Portfolios." PDF Presentation, Russell Investments Financial Services, LLC, February 2023

The table above points out some interesting facts. The white arrow in each row indicates the best-performing asset class for that year. As you can see, no one asset class ever outperformed another consistently.

Also, if you follow the column for bonds and compare it to the others, its performance does not have the large ups and downs that the others demonstrate.

Stocks lose money—sometimes a lot of money. Generally, adding other asset classes to your investments such as fixed income (bonds) can lessen your losses when stocks are down. However, allocating a portion of the investments to bonds will lower the anticipated return. In the story, $2,000,000 was enough to make the point. In the actual calculation, the result is about $2,145,000. By adding bonds and removing a portion going to stocks, we lower the anticipated return to 7%. This would change the result to $752,000 approximately. Roughly $1,400,000 less than an all-stock portfolio.

Comparing Single-Asset to Multi-Asset Portfolios

Asset allocation strategies (S=Stocks / B=Bonds)

	100% S	80% S/20% B	60% S/40% B	40% S/60% B	20% S/80% B
1977	8.41	7.34	6.27	5.20	4.10
1978	20.40	16.40	12.48	8.64	5.08
1979	17.05	13.99	10.98	8.01	4.80
1980	28.40	23.24	18.08	12.93	7.78
1981	-2.22	-0.46	1.28	2.99	4.59
1982	10.98	15.23	19.55	23.93	28.12
1983	24.23	20.94	17.72	14.56	11.40
1984	5.83	7.83	9.78	11.67	13.38
1985	41.76	37.58	33.49	29.49	25.93
1986	38.05	33.18	28.43	23.79	19.70
1987	10.97	9.96	8.57	6.83	5.07
1988	23.00	19.86	16.76	13.71	10.85
1989	19.00	18.21	17.36	16.46	15.53
1990	-14.42	-9.95	-5.37	-0.67	4.05
1991	25.12	23.46	21.74	19.95	17.89
1992	0.63	2.04	3.46	4.87	6.00
1993	21.53	19.13	16.74	14.36	12.11
1994	3.66	2.35	1.04	-0.29	-1.58
1995	23.45	22.52	21.56	20.57	19.52
1996	15.26	12.95	10.66	8.39	5.86
1997	16.88	15.56	14.19	12.78	11.14
1998	17.97	16.39	14.61	12.65	10.96
1999	22.11	17.20	12.43	7.79	3.57
2000	-8.01	-4.18	-0.25	3.77	7.45
2001	-13.64	-9.25	-4.80	-0.29	3.87
2002	-17.47	-12.16	-6.71	-1.11	4.41
2003	35.92	29.08	22.48	16.12	10.00
2004	17.23	14.64	12.06	9.50	6.85
2005	9.70	8.28	6.84	5.38	3.92
2006	22.02	18.36	14.78	11.26	7.70
2007	6.60	6.72	6.80	6.84	7.02
2008	-40.35	-32.73	-24.41	-15.35	-5.44
2009	30.50	25.70	20.83	15.91	10.89
2010	13.76	12.71	11.47	10.04	8.32
2011	-5.65	-2.81	-0.02	2.70	5.28
2012	17.58	14.98	12.34	9.68	6.91
2013	27.26	20.85	14.70	8.82	3.37
2014	4.31	4.73	5.13	5.50	5.65
2015	-0.37	-0.04	0.21	0.40	0.51
2016	7.59	6.72	5.80	4.81	3.74
2017	21.78	17.89	14.11	10.44	7.01
2018	-9.37	-7.40	-5.46	-3.57	-1.80
2019	26.16	22.65	19.14	15.65	12.17
2020	13.18	12.60	11.71	10.53	9.24
2021	18.50	14.32	10.25	6.26	2.24
2022	-17.46	-16.44	-15.50	-14.63	-13.72
Annualized Return 1977-2022	10.52	9.93	9.24	8.47	7.58
Annualized Standard Deviation 1977-2022	14.69	12.02	9.49	7.26	5.69

Figure 3 Russell Investments. 2023. "Comparing Single-Asset to Multi-Asset Portfolios." PDF Presentation, Russell Investments Financial Services, LLC, February 2023.

This chart reveals the results of mixing stocks and bonds into your investments. The first column consists of only stocks. The second column is 80% stocks and 20% bonds. The next three columns continue to add more bonds. At the bottom, the last two lines reveal the historical annualized returns of the various blends and the volatility (ups and downs) of each mix. As you add bonds, you lower the volatility and lower the return. If you do not like the ups and downs of stocks, you may want to add bonds to your investments. If you do so, you will need to save considerably more to achieve your desired outcome as bonds do not pay out as much as stocks.

Accept the Risk

Accept the risk until you have enough. Better to protect enough than shoot for more. In the meantime, however, do *not* try to time the market. This does not work. You must be correct twice—when to get in and when to get out. When the stock market rebounds, most of the gains usually come at the beginning of the rebound. Miss those days, and it will be very difficult to recover.

If you follow Suzie's example of systematic investing, you are dollar-cost averaging. This means when the stock market is down, you buy more shares. When the stock market is up, you buy fewer shares.

Resilience of the U.S. stock market

Figure 4 Russell Investments. 2023. "Investing Through Uncertainty." PowerPoint Presentation, Russell Investments Financial Services, LLC, February 2023.

What this graph shows is that the stock market does not trend in a straight line. While its overall tendency is upward, there are significant dips along the way.

Recently, the financial crisis of 2008-2009 and the COVID economic shutdown of 2021 are striking examples. Keep the strategy of all stocks until you have enough for financial independence.

Rule 4: Start Today

Today will never happen again. If, for example, Suzie liked the idea of starting her Roth IRA but decided to wait until she graduated college to start investing, the amount in her account at 67 would be approximately $700,000 less. The $6,500 she invested from ages 13 through 21 accounted for a third of the result. The power of compound interest over long periods is undeniable.

Retirement is often referred to as "The Golden Years" of one's life, during which one travels and has plenty of money to chase previously considered frivolous pursuits. I am not keen on retirement as a goal. I have always counseled my clients to invest enough so that work is optional. The sooner you start investing, the sooner you don't have to work for money.

SKIP AHEAD!

Too excited to continue reading?
Want to get started *now*?

Skip to Chapter 7 to immediately take action!

3
THE ROBBERS

Like everything in life, nothing comes easy. Often, we hit roadblocks on our way to success. Your finances are no exception. Inflation, taxes, debt, and time—if not considered or handled properly—can make achieving financial independence more difficult.

Inflation: The Silent Robber

I was born in 1942. As a lad, my friends and I would be dropped off at the local movie theater most Saturday afternoons. Mom would give me a quarter to cover the cost of the ticket, a drink, and a candy bar or popcorn. Today, I would need to pay 40 to 60 times more than that!

For our quarter, we saw "Movietone News," several cartoons, and an episode movie that always ended with a cliffhanger. Superman was trapped in a room with kryptonite, or the Lone Ranger had stepped in quicksand. You had to come back next week to see if your hero survived.

I also remember purchasing postage stamps for 3 cents and a gallon of gas for 35 cents. We paid the same amount for our first home in 1975 as we did for the car we recently purchased.

So, why have things gotten more expensive?

Inflation.

Inflation is a "silent" robber historically averaging 3.7%. If we applied inflation to Suzie's finances, the present value (purchasing power) of her $2,145,000 would be about $302,000. It is important to note that Suzie's investment grew over a 54-year period during which time inflation rates rose and fell and the cost of living steadily climbed.

Have you ever heard the fable of the frog? Drop a frog in boiling water, and it will jump right out. Instead, drop a frog in cool water and slowly turn the heat up to boil. The frog won't notice and it will be cooked to death. It is easy not to notice the slow erosion of the purchasing power of money.

In today's world, depending on an individual's lifestyle and debt, once a person or a couple starts taking Social Security, $500,000 to $1,000,000 may be required for a secure retirement. Social Security was never intended to provide 100% of one's retirement needs. This means that your Social Security benefit will need to be supplemented by taking additional money from your investments. Projecting 50-plus years from now, I would expect those numbers to quadruple to a range of $2,000,000 to $4,000,000.

This now sounds as if the task is way more difficult. Not so. In the Willie and Suzie story, I did not adjust her contributions for inflation or include her 401(k) plan that her employer provided. If you follow Suzie's example, you will be fine. Just make sure you adjust your savings to keep pace with inflation.

Debt

Borrowing money is a part of our financial lives. Some purchases are too large to pay for with cash. Limit your borrowing to large purchases that are actual needs like a home, a car, and education. Unless you are born into a wealthy family that pays for everything, you are going to be dealing with loans. Because most 13-to-19-year-olds aren't going to be taking on car or bank loans or mortgages, I'm going to limit our discussion to just credit cards and student loans.

Credit Cards

Most routine or subscription purchases are made with credit cards. It seems that my generation is the only group left that carries cash. In my 30-plus years as a financial planner working with individuals and couples, the ones who struggled the most to achieve financial independence were those who mishandled credit cards. Credit cards can be the cause of financial stress.

Therefore, do *not* carry balances on credit cards. That is, don't run up the balance on your credit card and then only pay the minimum monthly payment. The average interest rate on credit card balances is 18 to 20%. These kinds of interest rates are devastating.

Pretend your credit card has a limit of $10,000 and you use it all up preparing for a graduation trip to Hawaii with a group of girlfriends. If your credit card has an annual percentage rate of 18%, each month that balance sits out there, it accrues $150 in interest.

If you begin paying off the credit card balance at $300 per month, it will take you approximately 47 months to pay it off.

During that time, you will have had to pay about $3,967 in interest.[5]

If you pay $200 per month on the balance, the payoff period will last 62 months and you will have paid approximately $5,386 in interest.[6]

Do not be enticed by cards that advertise zero-percent interest for the first year. They are hoping to attract people who will run up balances. Credit card companies know from experience that they will make up for the "free" in a big way later.

Of course, there are other ways to get out of credit card debt. These ways require more discipline than most are willing or capable of putting in.

Debt Consolidation

Debt consolidation is a form of debt refinancing that allows you to take on a loan to pay off credit card debt. Essentially, you take out one loan to pay off multiple others (i.e., if you have more than one credit card or owe money in more ways than one).

This only works if you create a budget that does not require the use of credit cards or that uses credit cards, but you are able to pay the balance off in full every month.

Payment Styles

If you hold multiple credit cards, you can pursue a different method. While paying the minimum amount on large balances, you aggressively pay off your smaller debts. When the balances hit zero, you close the account. Repeat until you have no debt.

Again, like debt consolidation, you must budget your expenses for this to work. To ensure you never find yourself

---

[5] Experian, "Credit Card Payoff Calculator," Experian, Accessed June 1, 2023, https://www.experian.com/blogs/ask-experian/credit-card-payoff-calculator/.
[6] Ibid.

in such a situation, it is best to *never* put anything on a credit card that you cannot pay off when the statement arrives.

We need credit cards for convenience and to build a good credit score. A good credit score will help you acquire lower interest rates on large purchases—like a home or car—later in life.

Student Loans

The average student debt for federal student loans is $37,338.[7] Your monthly payments will be either 10 or 15 percent of discretionary income (depending on when you received your first loans), but never more than you would have paid under the 10-year Standard Repayment Plan.[8] Payments are recalculated each year and are based on your updated income and family size.

Assume you are a graduate with a $35,000 loan balance. Six months after you leave college, you will have to start repaying that loan. Not factoring interest rates into the calculation, you would have to pay $1,000 per month for 35 months (nearly three years) to repay that.

But for most newly-graduated students, $1,000 per month is an unsustainable and grotesque amount. If you were to pay $300 per month, it would take you 116 months (nearly ten years) to pay off the loan—and that's *without* interest earned!

---

[7] Melanie Hanson, "Average Student Loan Debt," Education Data Initiative, May 22, 2023, https://educationdata.org/average-student-loan-debt#:~:text=The%20average%20student%20loan%20debt,debt%20averages%20%20%245 4%2C921%20per%20borrower.

[8] Zina Kumok, "Student Loan Repayment Process: Everything You Need to Know," Bankrate, June 9, 2023, https://www.bankrate.com/loans/student-loans/repayment-process/.

Time: When Will You Have Money Available?

Previously, I discussed the importance of starting early and the power of compounding over time. Taking charge of your financial literacy is vital to investing in yourself! Most adults go through two time periods when they have the most disposable income—before they start a family and after their dependents have "left the nest."

In most cases, once children are grown and are no longer dependent on you, as an adult, you lack time to take advantage of compound interest as you've already spent at least 18 years tending to your offspring. That compound interest is not as effective as it was with the money you saved in the early years (prior to starting a family). But that doesn't mean you can't continue to grow your wealth.

Financial planning was my second career. I was never taught about the power of compound interest, so, naturally, I didn't start as early as I would have liked.

I was 48 years old when we had to close a family business. What financial resources I had at the time were used to fund my new vocation. Fortunately, three years into this adventure, I started to produce a positive cash flow. A few years later, our two children were fully educated and no longer dependent on us. Our lifestyle was never lavish, and we were able to put enough away so I could retire.

Running that failing family business was exhausting. My career in financial planning, however, was never work.

Do not waste time, or it will become a robber.

Taxes: Minimize Whenever Possible

Taxes are everywhere. There's a never-ending list of taxes that you are charged for every step you take. Here is a *brief* list:[9]

---

[9] "Types of Taxes," Debt.org, May 11, 2023, https://www.debt.org/tax/type/.

Federal & State Income Taxes
Payroll Taxes
Capital Gains Taxes
Gift Taxes
Inheritance/Estate Taxes
Property Taxes
Real Estate Taxes
Sales Taxes
Excise Taxes
User Fees
Sin Taxes
Luxury Taxes

You pay taxes on items you've purchased like groceries and gas and on services like internet or cable services. You pay taxes on utilities, vehicles, curbside orders, amusement park tickets, airplane tickets, Starbucks coffee, and spa visits.

Taxes are everywhere. They are higher in some states, cities, or counties and lower in others.

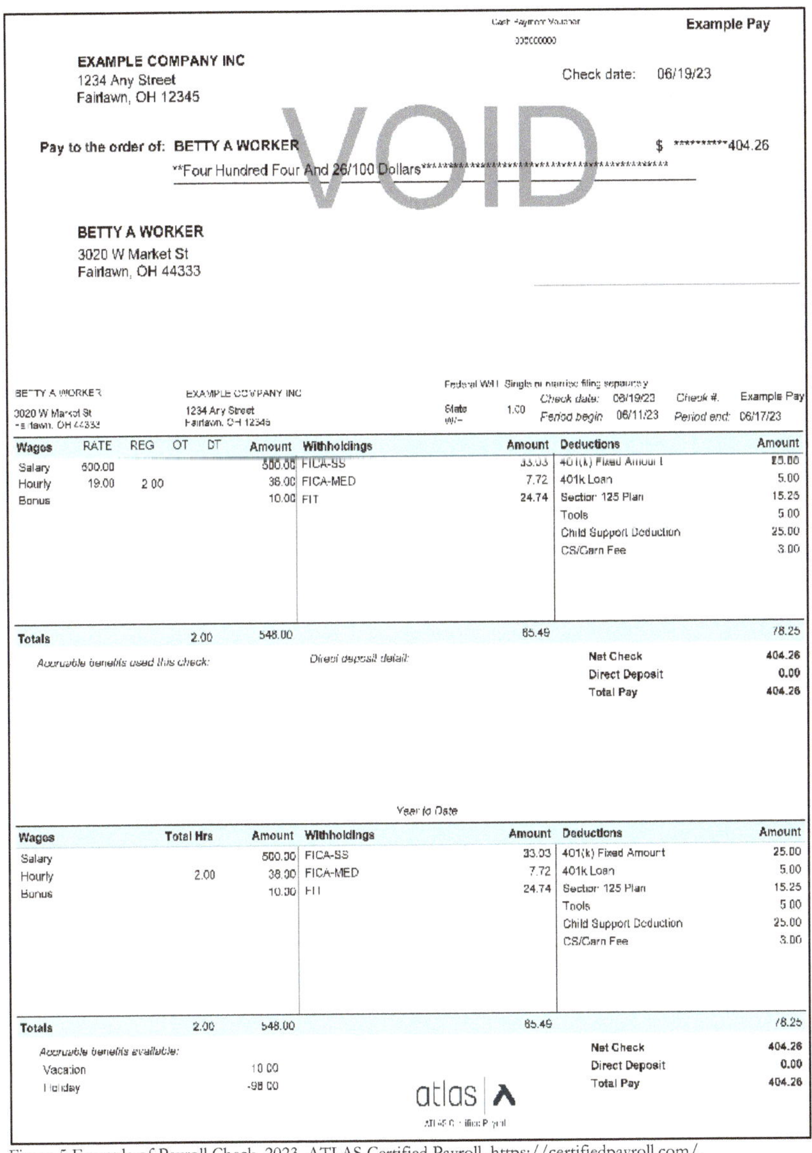

Figure 5 Example of Payroll Check, 2023, ATLAS Certified Payroll, https://certifiedpayroll.com/.

Here is a typical paycheck. Upon studying the paycheck, you'll notice the list of deductions included in it for federal, state, and city/county. In addition, there are deductions for

FICA (Social Security) and Medicare (health insurance for those 65 and over).

The good news for you is that young people with low earnings will be refunded some of the federal and state taxes. Currently, the federal tax on the first $10,275 of income is 10%.[10] Usually, more than 10% is withheld from your check. State income tax is different in each state. A few states do not have an income tax.

This is the rationale for using the Roth IRA over a traditional IRA.

---

[10] Sabrina Parys, "2022-2023 Tax Brackets and Federal Income Tax Rates," NerdWallet, May 22, 2023, https://www.nerdwallet.com/article/taxes/federal-income-tax-brackets.

4
UNDERSTANDING INVESTING

Discussing investment strategies does not thrill most people. It involves setting aside money for a future reward that seems like it will never come. To teenagers and young adults, it can appear to be an impossible task, especially when good-paying jobs for inexperienced graduates are in short supply.

As you prepare your post-graduation finances, remember to set aside money to buy incidentals or participate in fun activities and events.

Remember Suzie? She put half of her earned income into a newly-opened Roth IRA. She then spent the other half (a whopping $250) on whatever she wanted—trendy shoes, a new outfit, dinner with friends. She spent money guilt-free because she knew two things. First, she was on the road to financial independence. Second, her parents were her emergency fund.

Starting down the road to financial independence takes discipline and sometimes courage. An investment in a new PS5 game might sound great now, especially if Willie is pressuring you to buy it, but if it takes the place of your yearly investment, it is not worth it. It will take courage to tell yourself (and Willie), "No."

Choose a "Financial Friend"

If you have a life partner, share your ledger with them. If not, share it with a parent or a friend. Select a "financial friend," someone who is responsible and experienced and whose advice you trust.

This friend will not only keep you from diverging from your financial plans but provide advice and feedback on your spending habits and tracking methodologies.

Now, I'm not advocating that you share your financial progress with strangers, but having someone (aside from yourself) hold you responsible and encourage you can make all the difference. Get yourself a "financial friend" today!

Encourage Others

Every time I tell the Suzie story to my friends, I get the same response accompanied by a defeated or sad expression. "Why wasn't I taught that in school?" My friends are mostly senior citizens; it's too late for them to take advantage of the power of compound interest. But *you've* still got time!

Pass the word on to your friends, and you may change their financial lives. There is no reason that a young person cannot build financial independence early in their lifetime.

Suzie Invests

Now, for the sake of teaching, I am going to change Suzie's narrative. Instead of saving and investing from an early age, Suzie didn't learn about the "eighth wonder of the world" until after she graduated college when she was working her first job.

At this new job, Suzie's salary was $40,000 per year. So, Suzie put 25% of her salary into her 401(k), which is $10,000. Employers will match an employee's contributions into a 401(k) account up to a certain amount. In Suzie's case, her employer matched 3% of her salary. So, for every $10,000 Suzie deposited into her 401(k), her employer gave $1,200.

Age	Contribution	Employer Match	Balance
22	$10,000	$1,200	$11,200
23	$10,000	$1,200	$22,400
24	$10,000	$1,200	$33,600
25	$10,000	$1,200	$44,800
26	$10,000	$1,200	$56,000
27	$10,000	$1,200	$67,200
28	$10,000	$1,200	$78,400
29	$10,000	$1,200	$89,600

Eventually, Suzie married and had her first child. During this time, Suzie dropped her contributions to 10% ($4,000). The employer's match remained the same.

Age	Contribution	Employer Match	Balance
30	$4,000	$1,200	$94,800
31	$4,000	$1,200	$100,000
32	$4,000	$1,200	$105,200
33	$4,000	$1,200	$110,400
34	$4,000	$1,200	$115,600
35	$4,000	$1,200	$120,800
55	$4,000	$1,200	$224,800

Ignoring any raises she received and the interest her retirement account earned, at age 55, Suzie had $224,800 in her 401(k). After the kids were raised and left home, Suzie—the ever-loyal employee—returned her contributions to 25% of her pay.

Age	Contribution	Employer Match	Balance
56	$10,000	$1,200	$236,000
57	$10,000	$1,200	$247,200
58	$10,000	$1,200	$258,400
59	$10,000	$1,200	$269,600
60	$10,000	$1,200	$280,800
61	$10,000	$1,200	$292,000
62	$10,000	$1,200	$303,200
63	$10,000	$1,200	$314,400
64	$10,000	$1,200	$325,600
65	$10,000	$1,200	$336,800
66	$10,000	$1,200	$348,000

When you factor in the average annual return, which is the interest an account earns yearly, that amount goes up exponentially. If, throughout Suzie's working years, the average annual return is 8%, by the time she starts withdrawing from her retirement account, she will have saved approximately $6,677,000.

If you'd like to experiment and do your own calculations for 401(k)s or other retirement accounts (like Roth IRAs and traditional IRAs), feel free to use a future value calculator on the internet. But stick to the independently-owned ones, not the ones from mutual fund companies. I recommend any of the calculators from Dinkytown.net.[11]

Suzie Doesn't Invest

Let's run through a different scenario. In this alternate timeline, Suzie did not start investing when she was first hired. She rented her first apartment. She bought furniture, household goods, and a large TV. Due to the debt from these purchases, she decided to wait to begin investing as she needed

---

[11] Retirement Calculators, Dinkytown.net, Accessed June 6, 2023, https://www.dinkytown.net/retirement.html.

the extra cash at that moment. Before she knew it, five years had passed.

One day while eating breakfast, she thought, *I should probably get on saving.* So, she began contributing to her 401(k). Between the ages of 27 and 29, she contributed 10%; her employer matched 3%.

Age	Contribution	Employer Match	Balance
27	$10,000	$1,200	$11,200
28	$10,000	$1,200	$22,400
29	$10,000	$1,200	$33,600

Like before, she changed her contribution amount when she married and had a child. At the age of 56, she reverted to a 10% contribution. Those five years of employment without investing cost Suzie $56,000. It also dramatically increased the amount of money she would have in retirement.

Upon starting retirement at age 67, Suzie had $292,000 worth of contributions. Depending on the average annual return at the time she began withdrawing, the total amounts in her account fluctuate but do not compare to the amount she would have accrued had she begun investing when she was 22.

	Total Contributions	10%	8%
Began Saving at 22	$348,000	$6,800,952	$6,677,299
Began Saving at 27	$292,000	$3,396,785	$3,335,026
Difference:		$3,404,167	$3,342,273

There are no excuses. Start early!

Life's Four Stages of Investing

Stage 1: Young Adult Years

This period is defined by your ability to begin working. For some, it begins at age 13, like Suzie. For others, a little later. In most cases, part-time jobs held by teenagers are missed opportunities as their money is viewed as spending money; they may do with it as they please.

When it comes to building personal financial independence, however, these are prime earning years.

As with Suzie's example, about one-third of her wealth at 67 years old ($700,000) came from the small amount she put in before reaching the age of 22. We need to be teaching this!

When investing during this time period, I recommend individuals, like Suzie, invest 50% of their earned income in a Roth IRA.

Stage 2: Career Years

The next stage of life is your career years before you start a family. Your basic expenses should be relatively low compared to your earnings. You may have options for investing at work in a retirement plan.

During this phase, individuals should invest 20% to 25% of their income into a company retirement plan and their Roth IRA.

Stage 3: Family Years

You get married; you have a child. Maybe more children are planned. Now you must factor in additional expenses (baby supplies, furniture, health/medical bills, preschool or daycare, etc.) as well as plan for potentially major expenses down the road such as college.

During this phase, individuals should contribute 10%.

Stage 4: Pre-Retirement Years

This is the time after your children have grown and are no longer financially dependent on you (you hope). Your children have finished college, moved out, and started their careers. You should be in your peak earning years.

During this period, individuals should contribute 20% to 25%.

Just being aware of these stages is crucial as most people go through life too absorbed by everyday happenings to see the bigger picture.

Make a plan from an early age and follow it!

5
BALANCE SHEETS

Suzie created and maintained a budget for her monthly and yearly spending. Whether you're 13 or 40, allocating money for different purposes is smart.

She never put pleasure items onto her credit card unless she knew she could pay the entire balance off when the statement arrived.

She kept a balance sheet over the years to evaluate her progress.

Suzie's Balance Sheet		
	12/31/2023	12/31/2024
Assets		
Roth IRA	$267	$550
Checking Account	$200	$400
Liabilities (Debt)		
None	$0	$0
Net Worth (Assets minus Liabilities)	**$467**	**$950**

A few years later, Suzie's balance sheet looked like this:

<table>
<tr><td colspan="3">Suzie's Balance Sheet</td></tr>
<tr><td></td><td>12/31/2043</td><td>12/31/2044</td></tr>
<tr><td colspan="3">Assets</td></tr>
<tr><td>Roth IRA</td><td>$40,000</td><td>$47,000</td></tr>
<tr><td>401(k)</td><td>$66,000</td><td>$74,000</td></tr>
<tr><td>Checking Account</td><td>$15,000</td><td>$15,000</td></tr>
<tr><td>Home</td><td>$250,000</td><td>$255,000</td></tr>
<tr><td>Car</td><td>$30,000</td><td>$27,000</td></tr>
<tr><td></td><td>$401,000</td><td>$418,000</td></tr>
<tr><td colspan="3">Liabilities (Debt)</td></tr>
<tr><td>Home Mortgage</td><td>$175,000</td><td>$164,000</td></tr>
<tr><td>Car Loan</td><td>$20,000</td><td>$14,000</td></tr>
<tr><td></td><td>$195,000</td><td>$178,000</td></tr>
<tr><td>Net Worth (Assets minus Liabilities)</td><td>$206,000</td><td>$240,000</td></tr>
</table>

A balance sheet, also called a **statement of net worth**, reflects one's financial position at a given time. Tracking this keeps you focused on what you are accomplishing with your earnings and investments.

During the family years of Suzie's life, she compares the family's finances to where they were the previous year.

Here is an example of what one of those ledgers might look like:

Family Balance Sheet

	12/31/2054	12/31/2055
Assets		
Home	$309,000	$315,000
Rental Property	$103,000	$105,000
401(k) Spouse 1	$113,000	$157,700
IRAs Spouse 2	$39,900	$56,700
Cars (2)	$8,000	$32,000
Life Insurance Cash Value Spouse 1	$12,600	$17,600
Deferred Compensation Spouse 1	$10,000	$33,700
	$595,500	**$717,700**
Liabilities (Debt)		
Home Mortgage	$168,700	$163,700
Home Equity Line	$24,000	$28,000
Rental Property Mortgage	$48,300	$45,800
	$241,000	**$237,500**
Net Worth (Assets minus Liabilities)	**$354,500**	**$480,200**

*A second car was purchased in 2025.

6
Avoid the Noise

The worst producer of poor investment advice is television. Successful investors are those who have a plan and stick to it. This is boring and doesn't draw in viewers. Television programs that "specialize" in financial guidance need drama and controversy. The object of these programs is to create interest, not provide solid investment advice.

Beware of financial programs that declare they have a system to "beat the market!" What they have is a system to sell you a service and collect your money.

Take what your friends say about their investments as idle chatter. "I bought stock in ElectroWiz and I doubled my money." No, ElectroWiz is up by 50% and your friend is not offsetting his losses in other investments.

Cryptocurrency

We cannot leave the subject of noise without touching on the topic of cryptocurrency. Unlike stocks or bonds, cryptocurrency has no fundamentals.

If you invest in bonds, you know the interest rate and the credit rating of the company or government agency issuing the bond. If you invest in a stock, you can know the company's track record, the company's dividend-paying history, and its growth in sales and profits. Most currencies are backed by governments internationally. For the most part, we are familiar with a country's economic stability.

None of that applies to cryptocurrencies. What makes a Bitcoin worth 12 pizzas one day and 100 pizzas a month later? Buying crypto is gambling, not investing.

7
THE ACTION PLAN

First, open a checking or savings account. Unless you are 18 (it may be lower in some states), you will need an adult on the account with you. Deposit money into the account. Once it is set up, it will be used for systematic transfers to your investment account, usually a fixed sum once a month. If your parents do not object, I suggest a grandparent for the adult on the account. They are more likely to have extra discretionary income and perhaps make matching deposits. I have a standing offer for my grandchildren. I will match the first $500 if they open an IRA.

IRA vs. Roth IRA

Open an **Individual Retirement Account (IRA)**, which is a retirement account that is created by an individual, not supplied by a company. Contributions to a traditional IRA are tax-deductible, meaning when you put money in, you can get tax breaks in that year. However, when you began withdrawing at retirement, that money will be taxed.

A Roth IRA comes with no immediate tax benefit for contributing. When your parents complete your income taxes, they do not receive a tax break from it. However, when you begin withdrawing that money upon retiring, you will not be taxed.

Because of how IRAs are set up, if you withdraw from a traditional IRA *before* the age of 59½, you will be subject to a 10% penalty. While both IRAs and Roth IRAs have their purposes, I strongly recommend the Roth IRA for young people. You are generally in a lower tax bracket than you will be later in life. The tax deduction will be small and not enough to offset the benefit of tax-free distributions later. In addition, withdrawals from a Roth are more flexible than a traditional IRA. Currently, you must start taking withdrawals for a Traditional IRA at age 73 (soon to be age 75). With a Roth, there are no withdrawal requirements.

If you are younger than 18, you will need the assistance of an adult custodian to open a Roth IRA. It is best to use the same one listed on your checking or savings account. If your parent works with an advisor, their advisor can open this for you. If they do not work with someone, you can use one of the large retail investment firms such as Fidelity or Charles Schwab.

Every firm has different rules on minimums. Fidelity has no minimums and no monthly requirements. The account can only be opened online. Some firms may require $500 to open an account or $100 with a systematic withdrawal from checking or savings monthly. The monthly minimum may be as low as $25. You can also do this with any mutual fund company.

When opening a retirement account, you will need to provide your full name, date of birth, social security number, phone number, and address. You must also share all the same information for your beneficiary (the person who you want to receive the money should you pass away). If you set up reoccurring deposits from your checking account, you will need to provide your account number and your bank routing number.

Contributions to IRAs can only come from earned income. If, as in the case of Suzie, her first earnings were from babysitting, she will need to document the income and file a tax return.

Another bonus to IRAs is that they are not reported on the Free Application for Federal Student Aid (FAFSA) form that determines if you are able to receive financial aid for college. If the money Suzie saved was in a savings account, that money would reduce the amount of federal aid she would be able to receive.

Exchange Trade Funds (ETFs)

The final step will be to select what mutual fund or **Exchange Trade Fund (ETF)** to use for your investment. ETFs are another form of mutual funds. The only difference is the way they hold the underlying securities.

The main benefit of ETFs is they are tax-efficient which is not relevant to an IRA account. If you accept that you are willing to take on the risk of equities and target a 10% return, the fund or ETF should be all equities (stocks). If you speak with someone at a retail firm or a fund company, make sure they understand this. You can do research beforehand. All mutual funds and ETFs' performance records are accessible online.

You may wonder—why a mutual fund, not individual stocks? Mutual funds provide some benefits over individual stock selection.

Mutual Funds

An individual investor putting away small amounts of money to purchase stocks is faced with many obstacles that mutual funds overcome. **Mutual funds** were created to allow small investors to pool their money with other investors. This allows the mutual fund to hire professional money managers and spread out the cost.

Mutual funds typically hold securities, stocks, or bonds from 100 to 200 different companies, thus creating diversification that would otherwise be difficult for an individual to achieve. Most funds have a specialty such as U.S. growth stocks, investment-grade U.S. bonds, or emerging market stocks (think China, Brazil, India, etc.).

Mutual funds are also required to publish their investment returns. These are reported increments looking back at the funds' progress (or lack thereof). Some funds have a sales charge in addition to annual expenses while others do not. Expensive is just one factor in evaluating which fund to buy. The most important factors are long-term performance and consistency.

While the task of selecting a fund or funds may sound daunting, the firm you work with should be able to provide assistance with your selection.

Keep in mind that the money you contribute to your 401(k) and IRA isn't just sitting in an account. It's being used by money management professionals to invest in various stocks, bonds, etc. When it's time for you to start withdrawing the money, it is meant to be there, but the health of the stock market and what your retirement account is invested in determine the amount you have.

Now, if you become savvy enough, you can decide where your money is invested and you can dictate your wishes online on your account. However, there are limits. Without the support of a fund manager, you won't be able to choose what you want to invest in as the online choices are limited.

Nonetheless, the object of this style of investing is to invest in the best companies in certain categories, such as technology, infrastructure, and finances. This is called **active management**.

The alternative is **passive management**, also known as indexing, which "tracks an existing group of investments called an index."[12]

Consider the most-used index called the S&P 500. This index represents the 500 largest publicly-traded U.S.

---

[12] James Royal, "Active vs. Passive Investing: Which Is Better?" NerdWallet, March 17, 2023, https://www.nerdwallet.com/article/investing/active-vs-passive-investing#:~:text=The%20biggest%20difference%20between%20active,of%20investme nts%20called%20an%20index.

companies. If you buy this stock market index, you will own a small piece of all 500 companies. It is a capitalization-weighted index, meaning that the number of shares you own in each company depends on the size of all 500 related to each other.

So, if all the shares of ABC combined equal $500 billion and all the shares of XYZ company total $100 billion, the fund will own five times more in value of ABC company than XYZ company.

The fund regularly rebalances for this weighting; it drops any companies that are no longer in the top 500 and adds companies that have hit the top 500.

What an index really has is the ability to take most of the human elements out of the process thus lowering costs. Despite this, some actively-managed funds have outperformed index funds over time.

Here are some funds that have produced more than a 10% average annual return over the last 10 years:

Fund Name	Ticker Symbol
Fidelity Large Cap Growth Enhanced Index	FLGEX
American Funds Growth Fund of America	AGTHX
MFS Blended Research Core Equity Fund A	MUECX
Dimensional Funds US Core Equity	DFEOX
Dimensional Funds Equity ETF	DFAU
Goldman Sachs Concentrated Growth A	GCGAX

Please do your own research or ask the company that your family is working with to assist you.

Remember, an idea without action is just a dream. Go for it!

CONCLUSION

I tried to make this sound easy, but the reality is that, like life, investing is complex. You are giving up your current gratification for something in the future. Sticking to a plan requires discipline.

You will be tested. Unexpected expenditures will crop up. Suzie's family discovers a leak in their home's roof and is faced with mold removal and remediation as well as replacing the roof. While her parents deal with the $15,000 unexpected cost, Suzie uses her money to replenish the family's emergency fund over the next year and a half.

Suzie followed the Golden Rules of Investing.

Pay Yourself First.
Have an Emergency Fund.
Understand and Accept Risk.
Start Today.

Anyone with the ability to work can achieve financial independence. Unfortunately, personal finance courses have been taken out of public instruction. The exorbitant cost of college has created a system wherein students are encouraged to take on student debt that will follow them for years.

Invest early and save often. Pay off your debts as soon as possible and don't overestimate the amount of money you allocate.

Set yourself up for success by following the Golden Rules of Investing!

ACKNOWLEDGMENTS

My appreciation to Joe Heider—boss, mentor, and friend—for creating a work environment that allowed me to succeed. His help, guidance, and patience paved the way for me to be able to write this book.

My thanks to my wife Pat, my son Jason, and Ryan Heider, who took the time to read my early manuscript, make suggestions, find typos, and encourage me. Special thanks to my granddaughter Lucia Bonhard who provided illustrations used in the book.

To Hal Becker—author, renowned public speaker, sales and customer service trainer, and dear friend—for providing a road map for writing a book. Thank you!

My sincerest appreciation to Sara Schumacher of Russell Investments who provided me with great educational materials.

My enduring gratitude to my clients—families, individuals, and businesses that gave me their trust. Their shared concerns and questions forced me to learn and develop as a financial planner. They have been a big part of my life and career.

Finally, my gratitude to Kara Wilson of Emerging Ink Solutions. This process was new to me, and I do not claim to be a writer—just someone trying to get a message out to an audience. Kara helped give that message form and clarity.

ABOUT THE AUTHOR

After realizing the extent to which youth weren't being taught basic financial literacy in public institutions of education, Mark Bonhard decided to correct that. As a long-time financial advisor to a variety of companies, legal and medical professionals, and corporate executives, Mark began utilizing his experience to teach the Golden Rules of Investing.

Mark has taught financial fundamentals at countless educational seminars over the years, focusing on topics such as college funding, personal financial planning, and legacy planning for colleges and universities.

Mark is a graduate of the University of Pennsylvania's Wharton School of Business where he studied economics. He holds a number of certified titles (all of which you won't care about) and is a member of a handful of professional organizations (again, all of which you probably won't care about).

If you have financial questions, Mark can be reached at www.goldenrulesofinvesting.com.